Summoning Spirit

Modern Haiku

Maga Jackson-Triche

Summoning Spirit:
Modern Haiku

Copyright © 2025 Maga Jackson-Triche.

Maga Jackson-Triche has asserted her right to be identified as the author of this work. All rights are reserved, including the right to reproduce this book, or portions thereof, in any form. Reviewers may quote brief passages. Artificial Intelligence (AI) use of this material is strictly prohibited.

Cover and Interior Illustrations by Maga Jackson-Triche
Book Design by Jeremy Berg

Published by Lorian Press LLC
Coloma, Michigan

ISBN: 978-1-939790-73-6

Jackson-Triche/Maga
Summoning Spirit: Modern Haiku/Maga Jackson-Triche

First Print Edition: January 2025

Printed in the United States of America,
United Kingdom and Australia

www.lorian.org

Dedication:

I dedicate this volume to my husband, David, our sons James and Henry, our daughter-in-law Alicia, and our grandchildren Kevin, Naomi and Isaac

Introduction

Writing haiku, for me, is a contemplative spiritual practice, one where I attempt deep exploration of my experiences and observations. Sometimes words come to me during meditation, but not always. Insight can happen as I walk down the street. It's hard to know exactly when and how my haiku poems begin. The writing down of the words and phrases becomes a process of distillation, with the finished haiku becoming a record of, to use David Spangler's term, my "felt sense" of my experience. Each moment of personal perception feels like a gift. My hope is that when you read these poems, you will share my experience.

A word about the structure of my haiku. I use the formal, traditional haiku poem structure which dictates that the entire poem have a total of 17 syllables; three lines with 5 syllables in the first line, 7 syllables in the second line, and 5 syllables in the third line. I have found that the structure gives me a sense of freedom. It's as if the structure is a skeleton that allows the "body" of perception to move and play.

The poems in this collection are divided into four sections: Encountering Spirit, Fellow Creatures, Seasons and Weather, and Eclectic Musings. Haiku, generally do not have titles. Readers are given the gift of discovering the meaning for themselves. So, in the volume, the poems are numbered.

Encountering Spirit

1.

I am a deep breath
At the still point of the wind
That moves through my life

2.

Summoning Presence
She comes in many guises
Waiting to be known

3.

Small acts of kindness
Echo through the Universe
Sowing seeds of Light

4.

Weave a lighted path
So that others may follow
Sacred stepping stones

5.

There is Sentience
Here and everywhere around
And it calls my name

6.

a.
About betrayal-
Forgiveness is essential
Though so very hard

b.
The true alchemy
Being able to forgive
Without forgetting

7.

In quiet silence
In a language before words
My Soul sings to me

8.

I am right here, now
Stretching toward an open hand
Reaching to grasp mine

9.

Open up, breathe deep
You are not in danger here
Learn to rest and trust

10.

Now, with wings unfurled
Deep inner rivers undammed
I emerge as me

11.

In sound and silence
A blossoming awareness
of worlds deep inside

12.

This is what I want,
A felt sense of the Sacred
Moving through my day

13.

This silence sinks deep
And whispers to my true self
"Choose the ancient path"

14.

Quieting stillness
An incubating cauldron of
Fire and soft air

15.

This very moment
This turbulent rough of now
Hones true mastery

16.

Being, not trying
Gentle doing, not forcing
Learning ways to love

17.

Profound Presence here
In this dappled, holy light
That walks and breathes me

18.

Beneath what is heard
Dwells a deepening rhythm
Sounding out true words

19.

Deep calls out to deep
Then listens at the bright edge
Where sand becomes sea

20.

I want to wander
Unhurried, unburdened, yes!
With wild heart set free

21.

Marvelous wonder,
Learning to uncover joy,
Tending to our hearts

22.

Our shared sacred breath
Immanent and evident
Ever unfolding

23.

Such a Mystery
Sharing this ground of Being
You and me are we

24.

Deep intuition
This knowledge does live in me
Showing me my way

25.

Walking the long way,
Learning how to meander
Absorbing beauty

26.

Opening my life,
Dissolving these straightjackets
Sewn of old thoughtforms

27.

Aligning with Light
Connecting with Clarity
Forging bright channels

28.

I watch that leaf fall
Can this be a metaphor?
Change is letting go

29.

Despite what we see
The sun is ever present
Even in the dark

30.

Let my hands and mouth
Become instruments of Love
Each moment, each day

31.

Of sound and silence
Yin and Yang of all born things
So still, yet moving

32.

Darkness can comfort,
Can enfold me like thick quilts
Can incubate Light

33.

No other moment
Is as important as this
Because, this is now

34.

There is no nothing
All that is, simply is
Revealed, or hidden

Fellow Creatures

35.

Even past midnight
I hear sea lions calling
What are they saying?

36.

Two gossiping crows
Side by side on that tree branch
Clearly, dear old friends

37.

Fly at the window
No open doors. It's winter
How did you get in?

38.

At the horizon
Birds swirl in tight formation
Soaring, heading south

39.

Two Canada geese
Flying alone, together
Dipping through the clouds

40.

Pigeons gossiping,
They are talking about us
And with great disdain!

41.

Other animals
Seem not to worry and fret—
So unlike humans

Seasons and Weather

42.

Sacramento Spring
Bright sun on flooding rice fields
Each seed a sutra

43.

Raindrops on windows
Mellow sounds of what's leaving
Echoes of what's gone

44.

This gracious moment
Light embracing, warming space
culling the shadows

45.

The sting of cold air
dusk, blue shadows, no fireflies
warmth beckons me home

46.

spring blossoms quiver
as their spent petals let go
then flutter away

47.

if I could I would
jump in puddles with bare feet
and savor the splash

48.

Mid-winter morning
Thin skeins of ice on puddles
Waiting for the thaw

49.

Snowing in Denver
Flurries swirl and dip through town
Will Spring ever come?

50.

9 degrees below
Here is where the wind bites clean
And licks fingers dry

51.

Edged with fog and ice
Iowa's Mississippi
Trudges through winter

52.

Spent leaves letting go
Surrendering to the wind
Bending, shaping light

53.

Much cooler today
Watching the grey clouds gather
Preparing for rain

54.

Red oaks in autumn
When green becomes a bright flame
And then surrenders

55.

Intense and glowing
Leaves like bright yellow beacons
Ginkgo Biloba

56.

Mist on that mountain
From afar, it looks like smoke
Fraying in the wind

57.

Terrible longings
Like winds howling through the night
Ripping leaves from trees

58.

Before the trees turn
They take a deepening breath
Readying for sleep

59.

This ice-cold damp day
Why do I feel such wonder…
Why so much joy?

60.

What a precious day!
Dense harmony of rain drops
I can hear each one

Eclectic Musings

61.

Dry corn stalks rustle
As the wind travels through them
Calling out their names

62.

Trees sing, did you know?
They hum, and murmur and croon
Listen, you will hear

63.

The moon, not quite full,
Strides past my open window
Glancing in at me

64.

Not telling the truth
Will always come back to bite
With very sharp teeth

65.

a.
On your journey home
Did you tarry, pass by me?
Whisper in my ear?

b.
Your bones can rest, now
Finally, among your kin
Safe and welcomed home

66.

Like a snail, I am
carrying my home with me
Wherever I go

67.

a.
In the deep quiet
The train begins its slow dance
Singing to the moon

b.
Low sounds of the rails
Clackety clacking rhythm
Lulling me to sleep

68.

Morning foghorns moan
Calling through the grey-dark mist
Sounding their way home

69.

a.
Greeting me each day
My coffee cup is steadfast
Holding, offering

b.
Steam does not hurry
Neither does this coffee cup
My lesson to learn

70.

Lone boat on the bay
Sails hoisted to catch the wind
Bobbing and bowing

71.

Time, Illusory
Depending on perception
Short or very long

72.

And what have we gained
In all this hurry and fuss
Much less than we've lost

73.

Way too much time spent
Fretting about perfection
Much better to play

74.

I want to wander
Unhurried, unburdened, yes!
With wild heart set free

75.

I crave the quiet
Need it like soil needs water
And water needs air

76.

Holding this mirror
My grandmother's face is here
Echoing through mine

77.

My body and I,
Friends, learning a new language
Greeting our old age

78.

In this clear moment
I am happy and content
Needing nothing

www.ingramcontent.com/pod-product-compliance
Lightning Source LLC
Chambersburg PA
CBHW051607170426
43196CB00038B/2956